DISASTER ZONE
LANDSLIDES

by Cari Meister

pogo

Ideas for Parents and Teachers

Pogo Books let children practice reading informational text while introducing them to nonfiction features such as headings, labels, sidebars, maps, and diagrams, as well as a table of contents, glossary, and index.

Carefully leveled text with a strong photo match offers early fluent readers the support they need to succeed.

Before Reading

- "Walk" through the book and point out the various nonfiction features. Ask the student what purpose each feature serves.
- Look at the glossary together. Read and discuss the words.

Read the Book

- Have the child read the book independently.
- Invite him or her to list questions that arise from reading.

After Reading

- Discuss the child's questions. Talk about how he or she might find answers to those questions.
- Prompt the child to think more. Ask: Have you ever experienced a landslide? Have you seen the aftermath?

Pogo Books are published by Jump!
5357 Penn Avenue South
Minneapolis, MN 55419
www.jumplibrary.com

Library of Congress Cataloging-in-Publication Data

Meister, Cari, author.
  Landslides / by Cari Meister.
    pages cm. – (Disaster zone)
  Audience: Ages 7-10
  Includes index.
  ISBN 978-1-62031-222-3 (hardcover: alk. paper) –
  ISBN 978-1-62031-267-4 (paperback) –
  ISBN 978-1-62496-309-4 (ebook)
  1. Landslides–Juvenile literature. I. Title.
  QE599.A2M45 2016
  551.3'07–dc23

2014050209

Series Editor: Jenny Fretland VanVoorst
Series Designer: Anna Peterson
Photo Researcher: Anna Peterson

Photo Credits: All photos by Shutterstock except:
AJP/Shutterstock.com, 11; Corbis, 8-9, 16-17;
Getty, 1, 14-15; robbinsbox/Shutterstock.com, 3;
Thinkstock, 4, 6-7, 20-21, 23.

Printed in the United States of America at Corporate Graphics in North Mankato, Minnesota.

TABLE OF CONTENTS

CHAPTER 1
What Is a Landslide? 4

CHAPTER 2
What Causes Landslides? 10

CHAPTER 3
Deadly Landslides 18

ACTIVITIES & TOOLS
Try This! 22
Glossary 23
Index 24
To Learn More 24

CHAPTER 1

WHAT IS A LANDSLIDE?

Imagine you live in the mountains. Your house sits at the base.

Last year a fire killed many of the trees on your side of the mountain. This year it has rained a lot.

Suddenly you hear a low rumbling. You look out the window. Rocks, wood, and mud tumble down the **slope**.

It's a landslide!

DID YOU KNOW?

Landslides move fast. They can move up to 35 miles (56 kilometers) per hour!

A landslide happens when a large amount of rock, earth, and other material moves down a slope.

Mudslides are a kind of landslide. They happen when there has been a lot of rain. The rain mixes with **debris**. It makes a **slurry**.

DID YOU KNOW?

An **avalanche** is like a landslide, but it is made of snow.

CHAPTER 2

WHAT CAUSES LANDSLIDES?

Many things can **trigger** a landslide. Earthquakes and volcanic eruptions shake the earth. So do hurricanes.

debris

The shaking loosens the top layer of earth. **Gravity** causes the debris to fall down the slope.

Logging can trigger landslides. Trees help hold soil in place. When trees are removed, the soil is loosened. Ground that was once solid can give way.

Construction also causes landslides. If the land changes too much, it makes the ground unstable. Homes fall.

Landslides happen in many places. They happen in all 50 of the United States. Most often, they happen near mountains and **valleys**.

If you live where there have been landslides, be aware! There will likely be more in the future.

DID YOU KNOW?

Landslides are costly. They cause more than a billion dollars of damage in the United States every year.

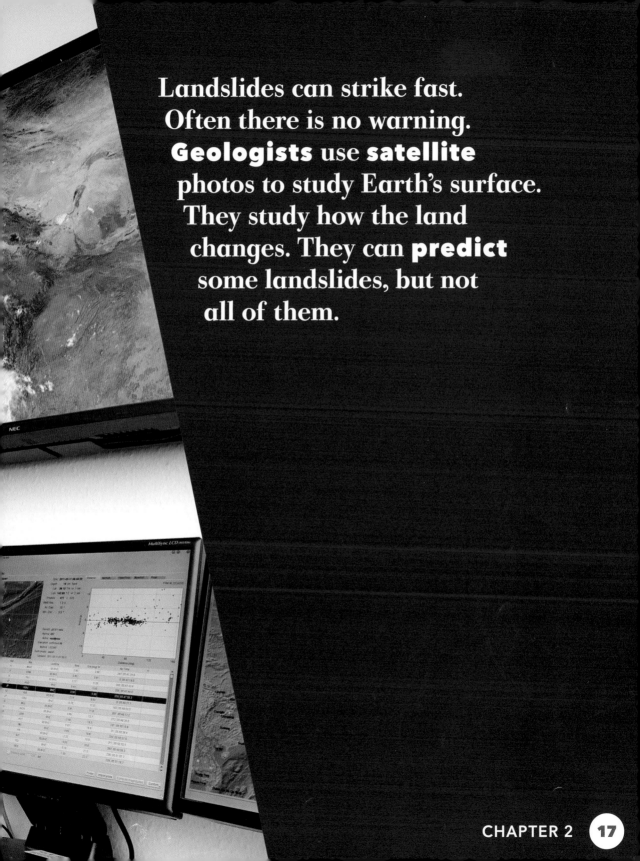

Landslides can strike fast. Often there is no warning. **Geologists** use **satellite** photos to study Earth's surface. They study how the land changes. They can **predict** some landslides, but not all of them.

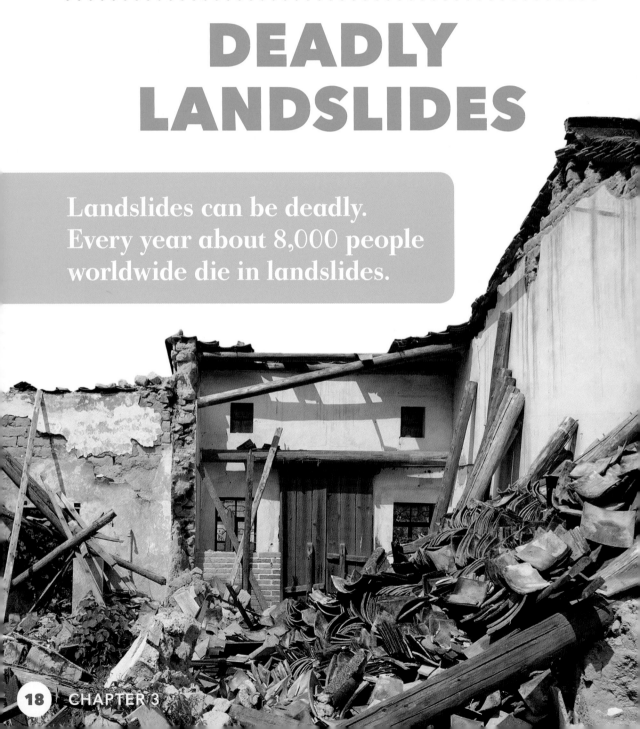

CHAPTER 3

DEADLY LANDSLIDES

Landslides can be deadly. Every year about 8,000 people worldwide die in landslides.

In 1999, heavy rains hit **Venezuela**. The rain caused thousands of landslides and flash floods. About 30,000 people died.

The most deadly landslides happened in 1920. An earthquake in China started big landslides. More than 180,000 people died.

If the news says a landslide may happen, stay alert. If you see one coming, get out of the way! Go as fast as you can!

Disasters can happen anytime. But be prepared, and you can stay safe in a landslide.

DID YOU KNOW?

An emergency kit is helpful in any disaster. It should include:

- Water
- Canned or dried food (and a can opener)
- First aid kit
- Cell phone and charger
- Radio
- Blankets

ACTIVITIES & TOOLS

MAKE YOUR OWN LANDSLIDE

You can make your own landslide!
This activity recreates the effect
of a lot of rain on a loose dirt slope.

What You Need:
- an outdoor slope made mostly of dirt
- a cardboard house
- a hose hooked up to water
- a sprinkler nozzle

❶ Find an area outside where there is a dirt slope and loosen the dirt a bit. If you cannot find a dirt slope, you can create one by making a hill of dirt.

❷ Put the cardboard house in the middle of the slope.

❸ Put the sprinkler nozzle on the hose.

❹ Turn on the water.

❺ Make it "rain" by sprinkling the water near the top of the slope.

❻ Watch how the rain makes the dirt move down the slope.

❼ Watch how the rain makes the house move. (This may take several minutes).

GLOSSARY

avalanche: A large mass of snow and ice sliding down a mountainside or over a cliff.

debris: Anything that a landslide picks up as it moves along; it could be rocks, dirt, trash, wood, or other things.

geologists: Scientists that study rocks and soil and how they move.

gravity: The natural force that causes things to fall.

predict: To guess about what might happen in the future.

satellite: A man-made object that orbits a planet; many satellites are used to photograph Earth from space.

slope: Ground that goes up or down.

slurry: Flowing mud.

trigger: Something that causes another thing to happen.

valley: The area of low land between two mountains or hills.

Venezuela: A country in the northern part of South America.

WATCH FOR ROCKS

INDEX

avalanche 9

China 18

construction 13

cost 14

deaths 18, 19

debris 9, 11

earthquakes 10, 19

emergency kit 21

floods 19

geologists 17

gravity 11

hurricanes 10

logging 13

mountains 4, 5, 6, 14

mud 6, 9

predicting 17

rain 5, 9, 19

rocks 6, 9

satellite photos 17

shaking 10, 11

soil 13

speed 6

trees 13

United States 14

Venezuela 19

volcanic eruptions 10

TO LEARN MORE

Learning more is as easy as 1, 2, 3.

1) Go to www.factsurfer.com

2) Enter "landslides" into the search box.

3) Click the "Surf" to see a list of websites.

With factsurfer, finding more information is just a click away.